GROWING UP
FOR BOYS

EVERYTHING YOU NEED TO KNOW

Published in the UK by Scholastic, 2022
Euston House, 24 Eversholt Street, London, NW1 1DB
Scholastic Ireland, 89E Lagan Road, Dublin Industrial Estate, Glasnevin,
Dublin, D11 HP5F

SCHOLASTIC and associated logos are trademarks and/or
registered trademarks of Scholastic Inc.

Text © Dr Emily MacDonagh, 2022
Illustrations by Josefina Preumayr © Scholastic, 2022
Cover illustration by Josefina Preumayr
Author photograph © Holly Clark, 2021

Produced with the help of:
Emily Hibbs
Consultant Paediatrician: Dr Rebecca Mann
School Nurse: Charlene Hayes

Dr Emily MacDonagh is represented by The CAN Group

ISBN 978 07023 1097 3

A CIP catalogue record for this book is available from the British Library.

All rights reserved.
This book is sold subject to the condition that it shall not, by way of trade or otherwise, be lent, hired out
or otherwise circulated in any form of binding or cover other than that in which it is published. No part of
this publication may be reproduced, stored in a retrieval system, or transmitted in any form or by any other
means (electronic, mechanical, photocopying, recording or otherwise) without prior written permission of
Scholastic Limited.

Any website addresses listed in the book are correct at the time of going to print. However, please be aware
that online content is subject to change and websites can contain or offer content that is unsuitable for
children. We advise all children be supervised when using the internet.

Printed in the UK by Bell and Bain Ltd, Glasgow
Paper made from wood grown in sustainable forests and other controlled sources.

1 3 5 7 9 10 8 6 4 2

This book is dedicated to all families who are trying to
navigate the journey through puberty.

To my amazing husband Pete, thank you for always supporting me.
Also, to our amazing collection of children: Junior, Princess, Millie and
Theo, who all keep me on my toes!

To my mum and dad who taught me pretty much everything you will read
here. Mum – I can't thank you enough for being my medical expert for this
book, although I think it was actually your parental expertise that helped
the most! Dad – your words of wisdom are invaluable to me.

Finally, to my little brothers (who are not so little any more)
Tom, Sam, Will and Joe.

I love you all xx

GROWING UP
FOR BOYS

EVERYTHING
YOU NEED TO
KNOW

DR EMILY MACDONAGH

ILLUSTRATED BY JOSEFINA PREUMAYR

■SCHOLASTIC

INTRODUCTION
WHAT TO EXPECT

This is a book all about growing up and the sorts of
things that might happen to you during your teenage years:
the good bits, the embarrassing bits, the confusing bits and the
tough bits. Right now, you might be wondering whether you're
ready for the changes coming your way. Over the following
chapters, I'm going to give you the tools, knowledge and
know-how you need to be as prepared as possible. By the
final page, you should feel clued-up and confident
about what's ahead!

You've probably heard your parents or teachers talking about puberty. You might already know lots about it, or maybe you're a bit puzzled. Basically, puberty just means all the changes your body will go through to transform from a child into a teenager into an adult. Over the next few years, you'll start to notice your body looking and feeling different. In this book, I'll talk you through the changes – big and small – that are coming. Getting to grips with what your body might do before it starts doing it will mean there's no reason to feel worried or confused when things begin to happen.

NICE TO MEET YOU!

I'm **DR EMILY**, and I work for the National Health Service (NHS). I went to university for five years to study medicine, where I learned all about the changes children and young people go through during puberty. Then I started working as a doctor, which I have done for the last six years. I have worked in all sorts of places, and have loved meeting so many different people. Being a doctor can be tough, but it is also an amazing job because you can help people at difficult times in their lives.

I have a whopping FOUR younger brothers, who I watched grow up. As their older sister, I saw each one of them going through puberty… I got used to being asked lots of questions and found out all about which bits were difficult or confusing for them. I have also seen my two stepchildren growing from infancy to Instagram! I am now bringing up my own children and I have really sussed out the easy bits and the hard bits about growing up, along with the questions everyone wants to ask about puberty but are too embarrassed to… I've had lots of practice explaining how growing up works over the years and now I've put all that knowledge in a book so that YOU can find out all about it too. The most important thing I want you to know is that no question is silly or embarrassing. If you want to know the answer to something, chances are someone else will too. The more we speak out and ask those tricky questions, the easier it will become for everyone to get the information they need!

Over the following chapters, I'll take you through the journey of puberty, explaining the things that will happen to your body and why. This book is mostly about boys' bodies, but there's a short chapter about what's happening to the girls, too. Before we get started, here's something to keep in mind:

THERE IS NO RIGHT OR WRONG WAY TO GROW UP! EVERYONE GOES THROUGH PUBERTY IN THEIR OWN WAY, AT THEIR OWN TIME.

BUT PUBERTY IS SOMETHING THAT HAPPENS TO EVERY SINGLE ONE OF US AT SOME POINT OR OTHER, SO IT IS GOOD TO KNOW WHAT IS COMING...

Whatever you're feeling right now, you're not alone. Every adult on the planet – from your grandad to your favourite footballer – has been through the process of puberty. Growing up is great. Really. In less than ten years' time, you will have finished school and can live with your friends or go travelling. You can land your dream job, earn your own money and choose how to spend it. You've got an amazing, exciting adventure ahead of you. Are you ready to get started?

WHAT'S THE POINT OF PUBERTY?

As well as getting your brain ready to be an independent adult, puberty gets your body ready in case you want to have children one day. Though not everyone wants to have, or can have, a child, it's still important for your body and brain to develop. Over the next few years, the changes you feel inside are just as important as the changes you'll see on the outside. You'll experience new feelings and get to know yourself better, as well as developing new interests.

THERE ARE LOTS OF TRICKY TERMS TO KEEP TRACK OF WHEN WE TALK ABOUT PUBERTY AND GROWING UP. YOU'LL FIND A LIST OF THE MOST IMPORTANT ONES AT THE BACK OF THE BOOK IN THE GLOSSARY.

ALL CHANGE!

Here are a few of the changes boys go through during puberty. We'll look at all of these in much more detail later in the book.

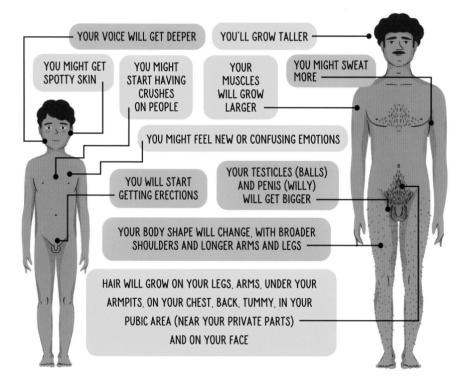

YOUR VOICE WILL GET DEEPER

YOU'LL GROW TALLER

YOU MIGHT GET SPOTTY SKIN

YOU MIGHT START HAVING CRUSHES ON PEOPLE

YOUR MUSCLES WILL GROW LARGER

YOU MIGHT SWEAT MORE

YOU MIGHT FEEL NEW OR CONFUSING EMOTIONS

YOU WILL START GETTING ERECTIONS

YOUR TESTICLES (BALLS) AND PENIS (WILLY) WILL GET BIGGER

YOUR BODY SHAPE WILL CHANGE, WITH BROADER SHOULDERS AND LONGER ARMS AND LEGS

HAIR WILL GROW ON YOUR LEGS, ARMS, UNDER YOUR ARMPITS, ON YOUR CHEST, BACK, TUMMY, IN YOUR PUBIC AREA (NEAR YOUR PRIVATE PARTS) AND ON YOUR FACE

Don't panic if that sounds like a lot of **BIG** changes – they're not going to happen overnight! These changes will happen gradually over several years.

DOWN BELOW

We're going to be talking a lot about things going on 'DOWN BELOW', in your genital area, so here's a quick diagram so you're clear on what's what. REMEMBER, EVERYBODY'S BODY LOOKS DIFFERENT – THIS IS JUST A GUIDE!

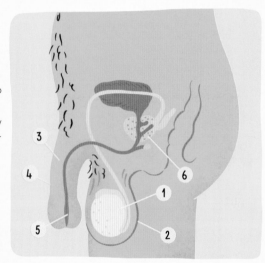

1 TESTICLES Two balls which make sperm. Sperm are special cells which, if they fertilize an egg in a female body, can grow into a baby. The testicles also make hormones (especially testosterone) which trigger changes in your body during puberty.

2 SCROTUM A bag of skin which holds the testicles.

3 PENIS An organ which leads from the inside of your body to the outside. You wee out of the opening at the end of your penis. It can also release semen (a fluid containing sperm) which travels up from your testicles through your penis.

4 FORESKIN The skin that covers the end of your penis – called the glans. (Unless your penis is circumcised – see page 22.)

5 URETHRA The tube through which urine (wee) leaves your body.

6 PROSTATE A gland which sits at the bottom of your bladder and produces a fluid that mixes with sperm to make semen.

And just so you know, here's what **GIRLS' GENITALS** look like:

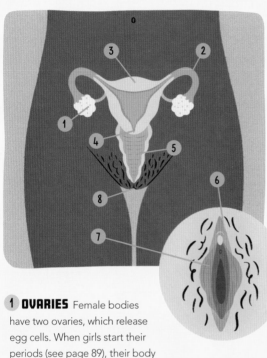

bigger as a baby inside it grows.

4 CERVIX The opening at the bottom of the uterus, which connects it to the vagina.

5 VAGINA A stretchy tube which connects the uterus to the outside of the body. During a monthly period, blood travels out of the body through the vagina. It is also where babies are born through.

1 OVARIES Female bodies have two ovaries, which release egg cells. When girls start their periods (see page 89), their body releases an egg from their ovary around once a month.

6 CLITORIS A small, round bump at the top of the labia, which is very sensitive.

2 FALLOPIAN TUBES Tubes connecting the ovaries to the uterus, which the eggs travel down.

7 LABIA Folds of skin that protect the vagina, which get bigger during puberty.

3 UTERUS (WOMB) The place in female bodies where babies grow during pregnancy. It stretches to get

8 URETHRA The tube through which urine leaves the body.

PART ONE:

CHANGES IN YOUR BODY

PUBERTY KICK-OFF

Puberty gets started at different times for different people.
When the brain decides it's time, it sends out some messages
to get things going. It does this through chemicals called
HORMONES, which act like messengers travelling around your
body. A special part of your brain, called the pituitary gland,
plays an important role. You can think of it like the manager of
a football team, telling each part of your body what it needs
to do and when it should do it. First, it tells your body to grow
and change in different ways. Then, it gets your emotions and
thinking to mature, too, so that you're ready to deal with
life as an adult.

HERE'S HOW PUBERTY KICKS OFF:

STEP ONE: Two small parts of your brain, sitting right in the middle, start things off. The hypothalamus sends a message to the pituitary gland which produces hormones.

STEP TWO: These hormones travel through your bloodstream to your testicles, where two important changes happen: the testicles start producing testosterone (the most important hormone that affects boys' puberty and causes other changes in different parts of your body) and the testicles start producing sperm.

STEP THREE: The pituitary gland starts producing growth hormones, which make your bones grow longer and you grow taller.

There are lots of different hormones whizzing around your body during puberty, all doing different jobs. For boys, **TESTOSTERONE** is the really important one. It makes your bones start growing faster so you get taller, and it acts on your penis and testicles to make them bigger. Testosterone also makes your body start growing darker hair and can make your skin more oily, which can make you prone to spots.

ASK DOCTOR EMILY

Q: WHEN WILL I START GOING THROUGH PUBERTY AND WHAT WILL I SEE FIRST?

A: Most boys start puberty between the ages of ten and fourteen years old but the exact age you will go into puberty depends on a number of things. For example, if your parents started puberty earlier, there is a chance that you will too. If you are heavier, you might go through puberty younger, and if you are smaller or if you have had any serious health problems, puberty will tend to start later. If you haven't started puberty by fourteen years old, this is often nothing to worry about, but you can ask a trusted adult to take you to your GP for a check-up, just to make sure.

For boys, the first sign of puberty is usually your testicles getting bigger and your scrotum getting thinner and darker. Pubic hair will also start to grow at the base of your penis. Over the next few years, the changes in your testicles and penis will gradually increase and you will notice other changes in your body (see page 11).

WHAT HAPPENS WHEN?

For most boys, puberty follows a fixed order once it has got started. That looks something like this:

1 You might notice your testicles and scrotum getting bigger and pubic hair starting to grow around the base of your penis.

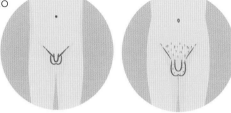

2 Your penis will get longer as your testicles continue to grow bigger.

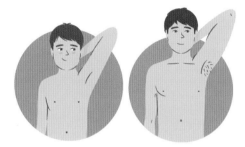

3 Hair will start growing in your armpits and on your body. It usually gets more noticeable on your legs first.

4 You might start to make a bit more sweat under your armpits, and generally get a bit more '**SMELLY**' when you're doing sport or feeling hot.

5 You might start getting spots, which can also be called acne.

6 As your voice begins to deepen, it may **'CRACK'**, going from high to lower pitches.

7 You might go through a **GROWTH SPURT** and become taller by around nine centimetres a year. Your body will also become more muscular.

8 Hair will start growing on your face **(FACIAL HAIR)** and you might need to begin shaving.

9 If you are going to grow chest hair, it tends to come last of all.

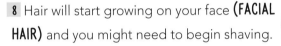

It is common to be curious about the changes that are happening. Everyone should take a good look at themselves in the mirror – it's how you get to know your body! **DON'T BE EMBARRASSED TO FEEL ABOUT AND CHECK ON THINGS**, or ask a parent if you're worried that something isn't quite right.

IN YOUR OWN TIME

There is a lot for your body to do during puberty and it takes about **FOUR YEARS** until you begin reaching the end of it. By then, your genitals will look pretty much like an adult's and pubic hair may have spread to the top part of your thighs. About four to five years after you start puberty, your growth will begin to slow down. Many boys stop growing completely at around sixteen years old. After that, it is common to have a few years when your height doesn't increase, but you may get broader as your body finishes growing its muscles!

Girls tend to go into puberty a bit earlier than boys. This can be a bit of a tricky patch, as the girls are racing ahead through puberty in their early teenage years, and boys can feel 'LEFT BEHIND'. Sometimes a bit of a gap can develop between boys and girls who used to be close friends in primary school. In the end though, EVERYONE CATCHES UP.

EVERYONE GOES INTO PUBERTY AT DIFFERENT TIMES.

There's no need to panic if you are the smallest person in the class and everyone else seems to be getting taller and growing facial hair. You might feel left behind when everyone else is having their growth spurts, but once they've stopped growing you'll catch them up, and may even overtake them. Some boys are PUBERTY SPRINTERS – first off the line and first to finish. Other boys are PUBERTY MARATHON RUNNERS and it all takes a bit longer – but everyone crosses the line in the end.

DIFFERENCES DOWN BELOW

One of the first signs of puberty is the skin of your scrotum (the bag of skin that contains your testicles, or balls) getting darker and becoming dotted with tiny bumps. These bumps are hair follicles (the place the tiny hairs on the surface of your skin grow from). Your testicles will grow bigger and, for most boys, one testicle hangs lower than the other. For reasons we don't quite know, the left testicle tends to hang lower in two thirds of boys, maybe because when it is forming, it usually comes down into the scrotum first. For no obvious reason, it is often a little smaller than the right testicle too! After the testicles have got bigger, your penis will also get bigger. First it grows longer, then wider. A boy may have adult-size genitals as early as thirteen years old or as late as eighteen years old.

Because we don't see each other's private parts, it's easy to worry that yours look strange. **I'M TELLING YOU NOW, THEY DEFINITELY DON'T!** Everyone's private parts look different, and there's a huge range of shapes and sizes! And guess what? **THEY'RE ALL PART OF THE NORMAL RANGE.**

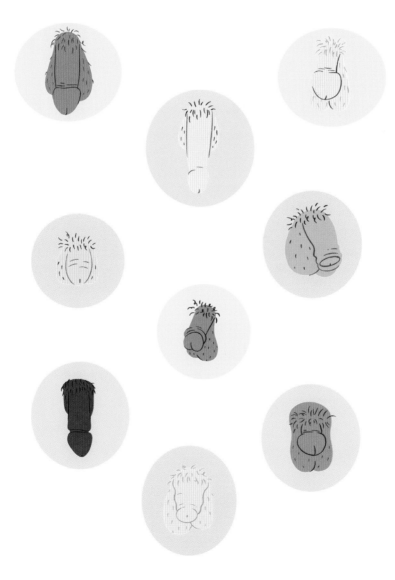

ASK DOCTOR EMILY

Q: WHAT IS CIRCUMCISION?

A: 'Circumcision' is when you have had an operation to remove the skin covering the tip of the penis (called the glans). As you saw on the diagram at the beginning of the book, the foreskin is a piece of skin that covers the round tip of the penis. When a baby is born, the foreskin is completely attached to the penis. Over time, the foreskin separates from the glans and can be pulled back. The age that the foreskin will separate from the glans is different for everyone. For example, at the age of ten around half of boys will be able to pull back the foreskin, and the other half won't. Most people will find that their foreskin will fully separate by the time they are an adult.

If the foreskin is too tight and can't be pulled back or gets stuck, the penis might need to be circumcised. Doctors might try other treatments first, before choosing to remove the foreskin. Sometimes boys are circumcised for religious or cultural reasons, rather than medical ones. For example, boys who are brought up in the Jewish or Islamic faiths may be circumcised, usually when they are very young. Whether a person has a circumcised penis or not, it is just part of who they are! It's nothing to worry about or judge someone for, simply another example of how we are all different in some ways and the same in others.

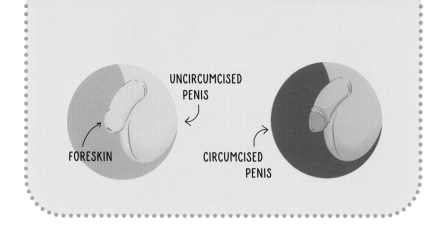

UNCIRCUMCISED
PENIS

FORESKIN

CIRCUMCISED
PENIS

DOES THE SIZE OF YOUR PENIS MATTER?

Lots of boys worry about how their penis compares to other people's. Feeling curious about a 'normal' penis size is common, with some boys worrying that theirs is smaller or bigger than 'normal'. However, it can really affect your self-esteem if the size of your penis becomes something you feel anxious about a lot.

Some people see a strong link between penis size and masculinity – meaning how **STRONG** and **MANLY** you are. There are lots of myths out there that 'bigger is better'. **THIS SIMPLY ISN'T TRUE!** Like any body part, there is a range of what is normal. Some people will have bigger or smaller penises than others, but that is just the same as someone being taller or shorter, or having bigger or smaller feet, or a bigger or smaller nose! **A PENIS IS A BODY PART LIKE ANY OTHER**.

If you are worried about your penis or testicles, including what size or shape they are, don't feel embarrassed to talk to an adult about it. They'll be able to reassure you that there is nothing to worry about.

Q: WHAT ARE THE BUMPS ON MY PENIS?

A: About one in three boys may develop tiny lumps on their penis. These have a funny name – pearly penile papules! These usually appear around the head of the penis. These bumps are completely normal and are not dangerous. If you have them, they are probably here to stay. You will hardly notice them though, and they are certainly nothing to worry about. If you are concerned, just visit your GP who will be able to reassure you.

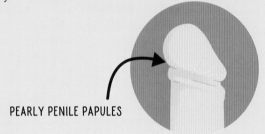

PEARLY PENILE PAPULES

THE ERECTION SECTION

You might have heard some funny names for an erection, but whether someone's talking about a **'BONER'**, **'HARD ON'** or **'STIFFY'**, they all mean the same thing. Boys' penises are usually soft, but during an erection, they become hard and start to stick out. This happens because the penis fills up with blood, like air filling up a balloon, causing the change in size and shape. Boys can get erections when they're really young – even little babies can get erections when their nappies are being changed. Erections happen more often as you go through puberty and become a teenager.

AWKWARD TIMING

One of the slightly tricky things about an erection is that it can happen at a time you are not expecting it. Boys often worry about this and think that everyone will notice, but that isn't true. Most people are busy concentrating on themselves and living their own lives, rather than focusing on someone else's trousers! No matter when an erection happens, it is unlikely anyone else will notice it.

One of the commonest times to get an erection is when you wake up in the morning, which is often when your testosterone levels are higher, and you're feeling relaxed. (Stress hormones, such as adrenaline, tend to stop erections happening, so you don't tend to get erections at scary or difficult times.) Another thing that can make you get an erection is if your penis gets a bit of extra stimulation – for example, being jiggled around on a bus journey.

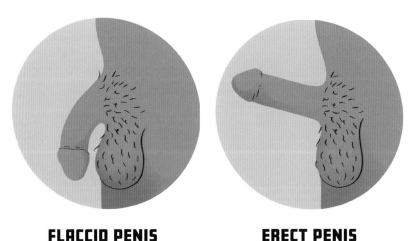

FLACCID PENIS　　　　　**ERECT PENIS**

ASK DOCTOR EMILY

Q: I'VE GOT AN ERECTION WHEN I'M OUT WITH FRIENDS. WHAT SHOULD I DO?!

A: Firstly, **DON'T PANIC**! If you have an erection in an odd or embarrassing situation – like right in the middle of a boring history lesson – there's no reason to worry that something is wrong with you. Your body is just acting naturally for a boy your age! Random erections are normal for teenage boys and adults, and given that you probably haven't noticed anybody else's, you can bet that no one will notice yours.

See page 28 for tips on what you can do.

Because everyone is different, it's impossible to say what a 'normal' number of erections is. Some boys experience several erections each day, whereas others may not experience any at all. Erections are affected by your hormone levels, which change depending on your age, level of activity and even the amount of sleep you are getting. As your hormones settle down after puberty, you should have fewer unexpected erections.

NO WORRIES

Still bothered about the idea of an unexpected erection? Here are some tips for managing them...

HIDE IT: Sit behind a desk, use a bag or jacket as a shield, or rearrange your trousers to help disguise it.

FOCUS UP: Think about something different. Some people find it helpful to perform a mental task, such as solving maths puzzles.

DON'T TOUCH: Make sure that nothing is rubbing against your penis. If it is further stimulated by you moving around or your clothes rubbing against it, an erection may take longer to disappear.

CHILL OUT (LITERALLY!): If possible, try going outside into the cold! Chilly weather can help an erection go down.

Even if you don't do any of the above, your erection will go away on its own fairly quickly.

WET DREAMS

If you've ever woken up with a wet, sticky spot in your underwear or pyjama bottoms, chances are, you've had something called a 'wet dream'. This is not the same as wetting the bed, and is a normal part of getting older. The medical term for a wet dream is a 'nocturnal emission' – this is just a long-winded way of saying something that comes out at night. A wet dream is when you ejaculate while you are asleep.

During ejaculation, semen comes out of your penis and this is the sticky spot you might notice when you wake up.

Sometimes boys wake up from a wet dream, but sometimes they sleep through them. You can't control what your brain does when you are asleep – just like you can't control what happens in a dream – so if you have a wet dream, you just need to recognize and accept that this is part of your brain getting more grown up, and that sometimes that affects your body, too.

Wet dreams begin during puberty when you start making more testosterone (it has a lot to answer for, that testosterone stuff!). Some boys may feel embarrassed or awkward about wet dreams, but they're an ordinary part of growing up. Most boys will have wet dreams at some point during puberty, and even occasionally as adults. They usually happen less often as you get older, though.

Your mum or dad will know about wet dreams – they were young once too! – so although it might be a private thing it does not need to be a 'bad' or 'secret' thing. Just put your pyjamas in the laundry and have a quick wash or shower before you get dressed. Wearing pants under your pyjamas may make things a bit easier too.

MAKING A BABY

I've mentioned that the physical purpose of puberty is to

get your body ready to father a child when you are a fully developed adult. The diagrams so far have shown you the parts of your body that are important during puberty, and some of these parts are important for making a baby, too. The parts of girls' bodies that go through changes in puberty, explained on pages 13 and 89, are also involved in making and having a baby. It is worth talking about how babies are made, because it can seem a bit confusing at first.

To make a baby you need a male sperm and a female egg. To remind you, sperm are the special cells that are made in the testicles, and can be released by the penis inside a fluid called semen. Eggs are made in girls' ovaries, inside their tummies.

To make a baby, a man and a woman have sex – the proper name for this is 'SEXUAL INTERCOURSE'. During sex, the man's sperm is released into the vagina. If a sperm meets an egg, that's when the egg can be 'FERTILIZED' and the woman can become pregnant. This is the earliest part of growing a baby. When grown-ups know each other well and are in love, sex is a normal part of a caring adult relationship.

HAIRY BITS

Humans are hairy animals. In fact, we have about the same number of hair follicles as fuzzy chimpanzees! When you're little, these hairs are so pale and fine they are almost invisible. As you go through puberty, however, you'll start to grow a more noticeable kind of hair on your legs, arms, under your armpits, around your pubic area and eventually on your face. Lots of men, but not all, also grow hair on their chest, back and tummy. Once again, these changes are triggered by **TESTOSTERONE**, along with some other hormones called androgens. The new hair is usually quite dark and thick.

WHETHER YOU HAVE LOTS OR A LITTLE, YOU SHOULD NEVER WORRY ABOUT YOUR BODY HAIR. Everyone has some, including girls and women. Many men choose to leave all their body hair as it is, while some others choose to remove or trim some, by shaving, waxing or using hair removal cream. Whatever you choose is completely fine and completely up to you! It is the sort of thing that comes and goes with fashion – sometimes having a beard is on trend, then a few years later everyone wants to have no hair at all. The good thing is that hair keeps growing, so you can change what you do with it whenever you feel like it!

ARMPIT HAIR

PUBIC HAIR

BODY HAIR

FACIAL HAIR

If you do decide you'd like to trim or remove any body hair, then spend some time looking into the different methods, and the pros and cons of each. Bear in mind that removing hair can cause rashes, ingrown hair (hairs that grow under your skin) and spots, so do it carefully and ask for advice from a trusted adult first. It's not a one-time thing, either! Like the hair on your head, body hair does grow back so may need a bit of looking after if you do anything too drastic!

FACE FUZZ

Usually, growing hair on your face is one of the later things to happen during puberty. Things will start off **S L O W L Y**. To begin with, you might notice a bit of fuzz around your upper lip or on your chin, or you might see a few hairs on your cheeks or around your jawline. Over time, more hair will grow, and eventually you might decide it's time to start shaving.

You might be interested to know that it's not only boys who get hair on their face – girls have it too. This is because testosterone triggers changes in girls as well. Girls' facial hair is usually finer and paler than boys' hair, though, as they have less testosterone.

Most boys will notice some hair on their face by around fifteen or sixteen years old. Some boys develop all of their facial hair quickly, but for some it takes longer. If you notice your friends have started to show off their full-on facial hair and your face is still only a bit fuzzy at best, don't worry! You will get there at your own pace. The other thing to remember is that, even when your facial hair is fully developed, chances are it will be different to your friends', in colour, amount and thickness.

This is exactly like other aspects of your appearance, from your skin colour to your eye colour to your height – we are all different!

ASK DOCTOR EMILY

Q: WHEN'S THE RIGHT TIME TO START SHAVING?

A: Lots of men shave their facial hair – they use a razor or electric shaver to trim back or remove the hair. The 'right time' to start shaving will be individual to you, and depends on several things. If you're thinking about starting shaving, it's a great idea to talk to someone who has already been shaving for a while, whether that's your dad, a big brother or an uncle. They'll be able to give you a second opinion on whether you're ready and chat you through what to do. They might even be able to show you how to shave for the first time.

The most important thing though, is how YOU feel. If you're feeling embarrassed, uncomfortable or self-conscious about the hair on your face, it might be time to start shaving! However, there's no reason to feel pressure to pick up a razor, just because some of your friends have already begun to.

CHOOSING A RAZOR OR SHAVER

Remember, growing facial hair often happens later in puberty. So whilst you might not need to shave yet, it's a good idea to know how to go about it so you are prepared. The two main ways to shave your face are with a razor or an electric shaver. I would suggest going with a trusted adult to a supermarket or pharmacy to look at all the different options. Remember, shaving needs to be done safely. A razor is extremely sharp and must be handled carefully.

RAZOR: If you choose a razor, you will notice that there are lots of different options.

DISPOSABLE RAZORS often come in packets containing quite a few razors. With this type of razor, you use it a few times and then throw the whole razor in the bin and get a fresh one.

REUSABLE RAZORS have removable heads which you can replace. You keep the handle and swap the head of the razor for a fresh one when you need to. These ones generally last a bit longer and are slightly better quality

than the cheaper, disposable ones, but either will do, particularly when you are just starting to shave and often don't have much hair to remove!

ELECTRIC SHAVER: Electric shavers are usually battery powered, so you have to charge them up, a bit like a phone or iPad. You are less likely to cut yourself with an electric shaver, but some won't shave as close to your face as a razor will. This might not bother you, especially if you don't have lots of facial hair. Like razors, electric shavers can still irritate your skin.

HOW TO SHAVE

Shaving is like any skill – when you first start doing it, you might find it a bit tricky. With practice, you'll soon get used to it and then, before you know it, you'll be able to do it easily!
IF YOU CHOOSE TO SHAVE WITH A DISPOSABLE RAZOR, HERE'S HOW TO GO ABOUT IT:

The best time to shave is after taking a warm bath or shower, so your skin is hydrated and soft.

Splash warm water on your face to stimulate your skin before applying shaving foam or gel. This will help lather the shaving foam or gel, and will make it more slippery when you start using the razor. It also protects your face by stopping the razor from being too scratchy against your dry skin.

Start by shaving the sides of your face, then the upper lip area and chin. Shave your jaw and the top of your neck last.

Move the razor in the same direction that the hair grows, not against the hair. This usually means going in a downwards direction. If you shave upwards against the hairs, this can irritate your skin and lead to a red or bumpy shaving rash, called **'RAZOR BURN'**.

When you have finished, wash your face with soap and water. **IF YOU CAN**, use a moisturiser to keep your skin soft and prevent irritation.

If you choose an electric shaver, some should be used on wet skin and some on dry skin, so do check the instructions. It's still a good idea to use moisturiser afterwards.

TOP TIPS FOR SHAVING

PAY CAREFUL ATTENTION TO THESE TIPS IF YOU'RE SHAVING WITH SPOTS OR ACNE.

- Shave slowly and gently, using short strokes at a time.
- Don't push down too hard with a razor. Putting too much pressure on the razor can make you more likely to cut yourself or make your skin sore.
- Make sure to change your razor head regularly, so the

blade is sharp. If the blade isn't sharp, you are much more likely to get a shaving rash.

- If you do get shaving rash, try leaving it an extra few days before shaving again. This will give your skin time to recover.

NASTY NICKS

Even if you're really careful, you might nick yourself while you're shaving. A nick is just a very small cut or break in the skin. It can hurt a little and will bleed a small amount, but often feels better very quickly. Sometimes you won't even notice that you've nicked the skin until you see it after you've finished shaving! If it happens, splash some cold water on your face, then find a piece of tissue and press it on to the cut until it stops bleeding (a tiny bit of clean toilet tissue is perfect for this!). There are some products you can pick up from a pharmacy which might help stop the bleeding quickly, including styptic pencils, specialist aftershaves or shaving nick rollers.

ASK DOCTOR EMILY

Q: HOW OFTEN SHOULD I SHAVE?

A: You should decide how often you want to shave based on how you would like your facial hair to look. If your hair is thick or dark, or grows very fast, you might need to shave every few days.   Many adult men choose to shave every day, or every other day. If your hair is finer of fairer, especially when you are just starting to shave, you might only need to shave once every few weeks. When you first start shaving, just use your razor on the areas with darker, more noticeable hairs. This will mean you don't have to shave your whole face right from the beginning.

Even though shaving can seem exciting and make you feel grown up, you will be doing it for the rest of your life, so there is no need to rush into it! The older you get, the thicker and darker your hair will become. As you get older, you might prefer to grow a beard, or keep some short stubble on your face. You'll then just want to trim your facial hair rather than remove it completely. One of the myths about shaving is that your stubble will get thicker the more you shave it, but that isn't true.

READY SET SWEAT

As you've found out over the previous chapters, our bodies can do some cool stuff. As well as being cool, they are also amazing at keeping cool. For everything to work as it should, your body needs to stay at around 37°C. Luckily, it has some clever tricks to keep itself at exactly this temperature. Sweat is one of the ways your body cools itself down when you start to get too warm, like when the weather is really sunny or when you are exercising. Your body's temperature can also rise due to hormonal changes, illness or stress, so your body will sweat more at these times too.

When you start to get a bit hot, your brain sends hormone messengers around your body to tell it to get sweating. Sweat glands, which live just below the skin, respond to these messages by mixing up water, salt and a few other bits. This sweat leaves your body through invisible holes in your skin called pores. When the sweat reaches the air, it turns into vapour and evaporates, like how a puddle disappears on a hot day. This process of evaporation is what cools your skin down. Interestingly, your brain produces the same hormones in response to other situations, such as when you are feeling nervous or stressed. That's why some people start to sweat before doing something that they might feel anxious about, like talking in front of a lot of people.

You need to drink plenty of **WATER** when you're sweaty, to replace the water you're losing through sweat. If you've ever tasted your own sweat, you'll have noticed it tastes salty. No matter how much sport you do, and how much you sweat, as long as you drink plenty of water and eat a healthy balanced diet, your body will sort out your fluid and salt balance.

STINKY SWEAT?

If you've ever been in a changing room, you'll probably have noticed a **FUNKY SMELL**. The smell we associate with sweat can be strong, and it's not always very pleasant! The interesting thing is that sweat doesn't smell at all. It's actually bacteria

on your skin breaking down your sweat that causes the **'BODY ODOUR'** smell!

While we might not always notice our own body smell, sometimes other people will, and might even decide to point it out to us…

If that happens, try not to take offence! Getting body odour is a normal part of becoming an adult, and there are easy ways to sort it out. You should wash with soap every day, making sure you clean under your armpits. Most people also use a deodorant or antiperspirant (which literally means 'anti sweat'!) to keep body odour at bay. A combination of the two is best, called an antiperspirant deodorant.

If you notice your underarms feeling sweaty or smelling whiffy, that's probably a good time to start using deodorant or antiperspirant. Deodorants add a fresh scent and just cover up any stronger smells from your armpits whereas antiperspirants actually stop you from sweating, or dry up your sweat. These products come as roll-ons, gels, sprays and creams and you can buy them in any pharmacy or supermarket. Most people put on an antiperspirant every time they wash or shower, so possibly a couple of times a day.

Some people don't need to use deodorant or antiperspirant at all. If you're lucky enough to be able to tackle your body odour just by taking regular baths or showers and wearing clean clothes, then don't feel the pressure to buy something you don't need.

The amount that you sweat depends on lots of factors, and is individual to you. Armpit hair can hold moisture, so if you have hair under your armpits it can make you feel like you are more sweaty. This sweat can lead to body odour, as more sweat means more bacteria breaking it down. This doesn't mean you need to remove the hair from your armpits though. As long as you are washing daily and using deodorant if you need to then having armpit hair shouldn't lead to having smelly armpits.

Some people do sweat much more than others. If you are worried about this, mention it to your parent or carer. You can see your GP or family doctor to get some help to make it easier to manage.

CLEAN AND FRESH

To keep sweats and smells in control as you go through puberty, it's important to stay on top of your personal hygiene. That means having a bath or a shower every day using mild soap and warm water. This will help to clear away any bacteria, so your body feels, smells and stays fresh.

When it comes to your private parts, you should **GENTLY WASH** your penis with warm water every day. If you have a foreskin, you'll need to pull it back gently to wash underneath, otherwise smegma may build up there. Smegma is a whiteish substance, made up of dead skin cells. It's found on the glans and under the foreskin. It is completely normal and natural to have some smegma, and even helps to keep the penis moist. If it builds up too much, however, it can start to smell and stop you from being able to easily pull your foreskin back. Smegma can even cause bacteria to grow, which can lead to redness and swelling of the head of your penis.

DON'T TRY TO PULL BACK THE FORESKIN IF IT IS UNCOMFORTABLE, as this could be painful. If you are worried that your foreskin might be too tight or stuck in one position, speak to a trusted adult so they can help you get advice from a health professional. See page 22 for more information on the foreskin.

While it is important to keep your penis clean, **SCRUBBING IT TOO MUCH CAN CAUSE SORENESS**. Washing your penis once a day, then drying it gently with a clean towel, is enough to maintain good hygiene. If you want to use soap, choose a mild or unperfumed soap to reduce the risk of skin irritation. It may be tempting to use deodorants or scented body sprays on your penis, but these are best avoided as they may cause irritation.

Finally, remember to also clean the base of your penis and testicles. Just like under your armpits, the combination of sweat and hair there can produce a strong smell, and tight underwear can make it worse.

CLEAN CLOTHES

There's no point having a clean body then putting on dirty clothes! **YOU SHOULD WEAR CLEAN CLOTHES, SOCKS AND UNDERWEAR EACH DAY**. Natural materials, like cotton, wool and bamboo are better at absorbing sweat than synthetic (artificial) materials like polyester and Lycra. But whatever your clothes are made from, you can still keep them feeling fresh and smelling clean! You just need to make sure you wash them regularly.

You should also change the sheets on your bed for fresh ones every one to two weeks. **THE SWEATIER YOU ARE AT NIGHT, THE MORE REGULARLY YOU SHOULD SWITCH YOUR SHEETS!** It's also a good idea to change them if you've had a wet dream.

HAIR CARE

Each strand of your hair has its own special gland which produces **OIL**. That oil keeps your hair shiny and waterproof but, during puberty, extra oils are produced, which can sometimes end up making your hair **GREASY**. Some people only need to wash their hair once a week, whereas others find their hair gets greasy after just a day or two. If that's you, there are some special shampoos made for oily hair.

When you do wash it, use warm water and just a small blob of shampoo to make lots of bubbles. Don't rub or scrub too hard, as that might damage your hair or irritate your scalp. If you want to use products to style your hair, some will add extra grease, which might mean you need to wash your hair more often. **IT'S A GOOD IDEA TO KEEP ANY COMBS YOU USE CLEAN TOO**, as otherwise they'll transfer grease and dirt back into your clean hair.

SPOTTY SKIN

As you've found out, during puberty your hormones
are going haywire, causing all kinds of strange changes.
Another thing they can transform is your skin. Just like with
your hair, glands under your skin release oil, also known as
'sebum', to keep it healthy. When you begin puberty, these
glands respond to the hormones rushing round your body and
start working overtime, making more oils. They are especially
sensitive to testosterone, and the more testosterone in your
body, the more oil they will produce.

Though these oils help keep your skin moisturized and stop it from drying out, they can also cause spots or acne. Spots can crop up anywhere on your body, including your neck, back and chest. However, the most likely place for them to appear is your face. A build up of oil and bacteria on the surface of your skin can make it easier for spots to form. These things clog up your pores, along with your follicles.

There are different kinds of spots, including blackheads and whiteheads. A whitehead is a pore that is clogged and closed on the surface of your skin. A blackhead is a pore that is clogged and open. Nodules are inflamed bumps under the skin that feel painful to touch – these occur when the pore is clogged beneath the surface. The bacteria on your skin can make spots bigger, more inflamed and sorer, too!

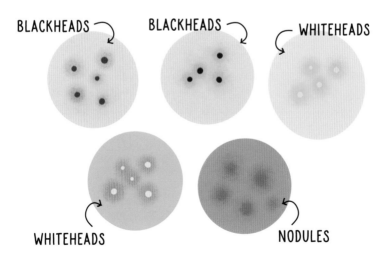

BLACKHEADS   BLACKHEADS   WHITEHEADS

WHITEHEADS   NODULES

ALL ABOUT ACNE

Acne is mainly caused by the hormone changes that are happening in your body. I had acne as a teenager, which started when I was about fourteen. I tried lots of things, like washes and creams, to try and help my skin. But then when it still didn't get better, I went to visit the doctor for some treatment. After that, my skin got lots better! This lasted until I was about twenty-seven, then all of a sudden, my acne came back! Now I am thirty-two, and still have problems with acne. One of the things that can make spots worse is picking them, which allows more infection to get in and can cause scars, so I try really hard **NOT** to do this – and you should avoid it if possible too.

Even as an adult, having acne has made me feel very self-conscious at times, always wondering if other people are noticing my spots. I just try and tell myself that everyone else is more interested in themselves and aren't looking at my skin. Or I try and focus on other things I like about myself. I wanted to share this with you so that you know if you are worrying about acne, you aren't alone!

It is so important to speak to someone if your skin is getting worse and it is bothering you. The earlier you get treatment, the easier it is to get rid of your spots. Acne is such a common problem – it's not embarrassing at all – and can be completely treated. Recently, I saw a doctor again and they are helping me try new treatments to make it better. So don't be ashamed – speak to a grown-up if your skin is troublesome!

Q: HOW CAN I STOP GETTING SPOTS?

A: Unfortunately, there's no sure way to stop getting spots, even though they can be easily treated. Almost every teenager has a few spots, and about one in five teenagers will have sufficient problems to need to see their doctor to get some help treating their skin. There are some things you can do, however, to keep your skin clean and healthy. This can help reduce how often you break out and how serious your breakouts are:

- Don't over-wash your skin, as this can dry it out or irritate spots that are already there. Usually, washing your face twice a day (in the morning and evening) to remove excess surface oils and dead skin cells that clog your pores is enough! You should also wash after exercise.
- If you use products on your skin, like creams, lotions or make-up, choose ones which won't block your pores, known as 'non-comedogenic' or 'non-acnegenic'.
- Keep hair gel away from your face when you use it, as it's likely to include sticky oils that can make acne worse.
- Avoid wearing tight clothes if you get acne on your chest or back, as they can rub and cause irritation.

PICKING AND POPPING

It can be very tempting to squeeze your spots, but it really is best not to. It won't always get rid of them, and may clog up your pores even more! You might even end up causing an infection, or giving yourself a scar. Your spots will go away on their own, so by far the best option is to be patient, and wait for a pimple to disappear.

If you're someone that just can't leave their spots alone, then there are some **RULES** to follow to cause the minimum amount of damage to your skin:

Always wash and dry your hands before touching your face.

Never try to pop a red, purple or brown spot without a 'head'. It will be very sore, and you'll do more damage than good.

Before attempting to pop a spot, rest a warm and clean flannel on your face for a few minutes, to help soften the skin around your spot, making it easier for it to just pop on its own.

FOR A WHITEHEAD, use clean tweezers to gently poke the centre of the spot. It should pop and drain away. If it doesn't, it's probably not ready to pop, so leave it be! Don't use your fingernails in place of tweezers, as they could damage your skin and spread bacteria.

FOR A BLACKHEAD, put cotton pads around your fingertips and press gently inward towards the spot. If the content doesn't come out, then stop squeezing. Again, the spot might just not be ready.

FOR NODULES: never squeeze nodules! They can become more inflamed and turn into cysts. See your GP for advice if you notice you are developing nodules, as sometimes they might need treating with things that you can't just buy from your local supermarket or pharmacy.

GET GROWING

At the start of secondary school, you'll notice that lots of the boys in year eleven **TOWER** over the boys in year seven. That's because, during puberty, you grow four times faster than at any other time in your life. You might shoot up by a massive nine centimetres in a year! In the first few years of our lives, we grow quickly, changing from teeny babies into stomping toddlers. After that, our growth slows down – until we hit puberty, that is. Then it all kicks off again!

A **'GROWTH SPURT'** is a time of speedy growth. Growth spurts begin when the pituitary gland – the football manager in your brain – produces special hormones known as growth hormone. Your brain mainly produces growth hormone while you're sound asleep at night. As you are growing and developing at a rapid rate, you need more sleep during your teenage years. More time snoozing means more time for your brain to get to work making that growth hormone!

Growth hormone mainly acts on the growth of your bones. In boys, growth spurts start with your hands and feet. One of the first signs of puberty is that you need to buy new shoes more often! Your hands and feet are followed by your arms and legs – there tends to be an inside out approach, with your shin bones growing before your thigh bones, and your forearms growing before your upper arms. The final part of bone growth is the chest and shoulders in boys, and the hips and pelvis in girls.

As your bones get longer, they gradually stretch your muscles and ligaments. This stretching is why you might find you get **'GROWING PAINS'** – aches and pains in your arms and legs. As your muscles and ligaments get tugged and tightened, it can be uncomfortable, especially at night. This will get better with time, but if you're feeling a bit sore or achy, try sleeping with a hot water bottle.

GROWTH SPURTS AND SPORTS

If you play sport, it's important to look out for growth spurts for several reasons:

INJURIES: sprains and strains can happen more easily during a growth spurt because your bones are growing faster than your muscles. That means your muscles can get stretched and strained more easily.

CLUMSY MOMENTS: you might find you're a little clumsier or less coordinated during puberty, as you're getting used to your changing body. You might even find you're more likely to fall, or drop a ball, while you get used to your new shape. This is partly because, as your bones get longer, your centre of gravity changes so much that it can cause a bit of unbalance while your brain gets used to it!

TALLER TEAMMATES: we all go through puberty at different times, and if you're a little later, you might find that classmates you used to tackle easily now tower over you. If you grow taller earlier than your friends, you might feel uncomfortable as you get used to your new body shape, too.

You can't really do much about your height, so it's best to find a way to be happy as you are, whether you're tall or short. **AFTER ALL, PEOPLE OF ALL DIFFERENT HEIGHTS ACHIEVE INCREDIBLE THINGS.**

BROADER BODIES

When you start to grow, you'll get taller before you get bigger muscles, so you might look a little gangly. Later into puberty, however, your chest and shoulders will become broader, triggered by **TESTOSTERONE** making new muscle cells grow. Your body will **'FILL OUT'** with muscle mass for several years – even into your early twenties. Before puberty, girls and boys have similar shapes, and similar physical strength. After puberty, men and women have different body shapes. On average, men's bodies are made up of less than twelve per cent body fat, whereas women have more than twice that.

CHANGING CHESTS

You might not have expected to read about changing chests in a book about boys' puberty. Men don't grow breasts (boobs) like women, but some boys will notice some enlargement of their chest and nipple area. This has a long name – **'GYNAECOMASTIA'** – and is a normal part of growing up. Some boys, however, find it hard to deal with and can be worried or embarrassed by these changes.

You might be wondering why this can happen. It's all because of those chemical messengers again. We've heard a lot about testosterone, but there's another hormone making changes in your body, called **OESTROGEN**. In girls' bodies, oestrogen plays a key part in puberty. In boys' bodies, oestrogen has a more minor role, but it can cause a small amount of breast growth. Even tiny amounts of oestrogen can cause some breast development.

One of the first signs of gynaecomastia is a small, firm lump under your nipple, known as a breast bud. This might appear soon after you begin puberty and can be quite sore to touch. Some boys can become anxious if they notice breast tissue growing. They might start to feel self-conscious and start wearing thicker or baggier clothes to cover it up. They may also find activities like swimming difficult, as they are worried about their friends seeing their chest. However, **HAVING A SMALL AMOUNT OF BREAST TISSUE IS COMPLETELY NORMAL!** It doesn't happen to everyone, but around one in three boys will experience it. So, if this is happening to you, remember lots of your friends might be going through the same thing.

Q: WHAT ARE 'MOOBS'? WHAT CAN I DO ABOUT THEM?

A: You might have heard the term 'moobs' – it's a shortening of the words 'man boobs'. It's not the nicest way of describing gynaecomastia, but at least now you know what it means! Most of the time, the only thing you need to do about any breast development is … absolutely NOTHING. It won't cause any health problems and most boys who develop breast tissue will notice that it goes away as puberty progresses – usually within two years.

If you are overweight, you might find that by doing a bit more exercise or eating more healthily, the breast growth will reduce. This is because cells that store fat can also make oestrogen (which is what led to the breast growth in the first place). Although for most boys, gynaecomastia is a normal part of puberty, there are some medical conditions that are known to cause it. If you are worried, or if you notice breast tissue doesn't reduce over time, speak to an adult you trust who can help you to see a doctor.

FINDING YOUR VOICE

Long ago, way back in prehistoric times, humans sometimes had to scare away predators. Scientists think that men might have evolved strong, deep voices to sound powerful and dangerous for just this reason! Today, it's unlikely you'll find yourself in a situation where you need to shout loud enough to scare away a tiger, but your vocal cords will still go through some changes during puberty.

Your voice is produced when you breathe air out from your lungs and it passes quickly through your windpipe to your vocal cords. These vibrate to produce basic sounds, and then these sounds are fine-tuned by your mouth and lips to form words.

In early puberty, testosterone begins to affect the growth of boys' vocal cords, and they increase steadily in size. By the end of puberty, girls' vocal cords measure about ten millimetres and boys' about sixteen millimetres. This lengthening of the vocal cords results in a deeper voice, which explains why men tend to have lower voices than women. The changes most often begin between the ages of twelve and thirteen, at around the same time as you begin your growth spurt.

Your vocal cords are in a part of your body called your larynx, or voice box. As this grows, it might stick out a bit at the front of your throat. This is called your Adam's apple (because it kind of looks like you've swallowed a piece of fruit!). Not everyone has one though.

SQUEAKY SOUNDS

While your vocal cords go through that time of growth, your voice can be difficult to control. It can suddenly drop, go very high or make other unexpected sounds. This is what people mean when they say your voice is 'BREAKING' or 'CRACKING'. These sounds are simply signs that your vocal cords are increasing in size, in line with the rest of your body. They will often be linked with a sudden growth spurt – so every cloud has a silver lining! Your voice might be changing in surprising ways, but you are likely to get taller and broader at the same time. The changes will settle down in time, and you'll have a level, lower voice.

Puberty can be a complicated time, and voice changes can add uncertainty and make you feel self-conscious – but hopefully by understanding what is going on and why it happens you'll feel reassured. The change in your voice pitch (HOW HIGH OR LOW IT IS) from before puberty and after can be quite striking. Some boys' voices drop down by about an octave, and that is why their singing voices can change so much. For an example of how much boys' voices can change, you could check out a video of singer Justin Bieber when he had just become famous as a young teen in 2009, and compare it to how he sounds now!

PART TWO:

CHANGES IN YOUR MIND

BRILLIANT BRAINS

Our brains are complicated places. Different areas of our brains control different things, from breathing to balance to moods. During puberty, your brain will go through changes, just like your body. You'll experience different thoughts, interests and feelings. Some of these changes, particularly the ones to do with your emotions, might make you feel like you are on a bit of a rollercoaster!

CHANGING MINDS

When you're younger, your life is ruled by your parents, teachers or other grown-ups. They make decisions about what you should wear, eat or do, in order to keep you safe, happy and healthy. By the time you are eighteen, and legally an adult, you'll be well on your way to being fully independent. Not only will you get to choose what you have for dinner or what clothes you wear, but you might also start thinking about getting a job or an apprenticeship, going to university or leaving home. During your teenage years, your brain will need to change and develop to get you ready to do those grown-up things.

As we grow, our brain is changing all the time. I'm sure you'll agree you're quite different from the three-year-old version of yourself. Back then, you probably thought:

"EVERYTHING IS ALL ABOUT **ME!**"

If you know any toddlers, you might have seen them have some mega tantrums if they don't get their own way! At that age, our whole world is made up of our family and close friends. But as we get older, we start paying more attention to the wider world. We might become interested in the news, or sports, or politics, or in people from different places or cultures. As teenagers, people often feel more connected and engaged with the world around them.

Your brain is made up of lots of different sections, which all have important jobs to do. During early puberty, the front part of your brain – called the frontal lobe – starts to get more powerful. It's the part of the brain that controls your impulses and stops you from making rushed decisions. During your teenage years, other bits of your brain also develop. They get you ready to try the new things you need to learn as you prepare to become an adult.

RISKY BUSINESS

Trying new things is often a great idea. We need to do it in order to learn to drive, cook or move out. Sometimes, however, trying risky activities without thinking about the consequences or dangers can cause problems. For example, if you've never skateboarded before, but decide one day to try out an advanced trick you've seen on TikTok, there's a chance you'll end up hurt. Or if you decide to try smoking or drinking alcohol without stopping to think whether it's a sensible and safe idea first, you might run into trouble there, too. Making a decision without thinking it through is not a wise move.

WE ALL MAKE MISTAKES FROM TIME TO TIME. But learning from these mistakes is what helps us grow into independent and confident adults. By the time the 'sensible' front part of our brain gets in full control, we've generally worked out our limits and can enjoy life as a grown-up in a safe and happy way.

Q: WHY WON'T MY PARENTS LET ME DO AS MUCH AS MY FRIENDS?

A: As you go through your teenage years, you'll want to make more and more decisions for yourself. You might want to travel on your own, or meet your friends without your parents, or stay out later. It's possible that you'll begin to put more importance on what your friends think about you than on pleasing your parents.

Everyone's parents will have different rules and boundaries, and yours may not be as laid back as your friends'! Do remember though, they've been through everything you're going through, and it's worth hearing them out when they tell you to do – or not to do – something. Their reasons are probably good ones! The most important thing is to talk things through. Communication is key to understanding where other people are coming from and may even help you and your parents come to a compromise.

MONSTER MOODS

As your brain matures, it needs to help you learn to assess and take risks, and to make more independent decisions. Those are really complicated skills! When we talk about puberty being an emotional rollercoaster, we're talking about the strong feelings you can develop as you learn these skills. These can include:

- mood swings (moods changing quickly)
- low self-esteem (feeling bad about yourself)
- aggression (feeling angry)

It is normal to feel these things in the run up to and during puberty, but it is easier to manage them if you share how you're feeling with someone. Have you heard of the saying, **'A PROBLEM SHARED IS A PROBLEM HALVED'?** It means that chatting a problem through with someone can help us put things in perspective and make us feel less alone.

Our mental health – which means the healthiness of our minds – is really important. Lots of people struggle with their mental health at some point during their lives. If you feel that you're not enjoying activities you used to like doing, that you're worried or stressed all the time, that you're having difficulty with sleep, or concentrating, or you don't feel like eating, then these are things you should talk to someone about. Talk to your parents, a teacher or a friend about what you are going through. There are also some phone numbers for mental health helplines at the back of this book.

FEELINGS STUFF

In the past, there was a lot of pressure on boys to act a certain way. Boys were supposed to be seen as tough and 'manly', never showing their soft or vulnerable side. Some boys still feel pressure to come across this way – but it's not great to hide your emotions like that, particularly if something has really got you down. Sometimes we need to accept that something has happened in our lives that has upset us. And you know what? **CRYING IS OK.** Scientists think that tears release chemicals which relieve stress and help us feel better. So, if something sad has happened, don't feel you have to pretend it hasn't.

As well as talking to somebody else when you're sad, remember to talk to **YOURSELF** kindly. When we're feeling down in the dumps, it's easy for the little voice in our head to turn nasty, and tell us we're embarrassing or useless. Instead, try to give yourself positive feedback – **FOCUS ON THE THINGS YOU ARE GOOD AT, AND THINGS THAT MAKE YOU FEEL GOOD ABOUT YOURSELF.**

ASK DOCTOR EMILY

Q: HOW CAN I CALM DOWN WHEN I'M FEELING ANGRY?

A: Sometimes, boys can feel a bit angrier during puberty. One of the reasons for this is that testosterone can cause aggression. When we're angry, the emotional part of our brain takes over from the rational part of our brain, and we can end up making some bad decisions, like shouting at our parents or talking back to our teachers. If you can work out that you're feeling angry before you fly off the handle, you can take some time out of the situation. Taking a few minutes to breathe deeply can give your rational mind time to get back in control. If your thoughts race off in an angry direction, just bring your focus back to your breathing. If you do this for three to five minutes, you should start to feel calmer, cooler and back in control.

FIRST CRUSHES

Another thing that might change in your brain during puberty is how you feel towards certain other people. If you find yourself thinking about someone **ALL THE TIME**, imagining getting close to them or even kissing them, chances are you're feeling attracted to them. If both of you feel the same way, you may want to start a relationship, sometimes called 'GOING OUT WITH SOMEONE' or becoming boyfriend and girlfriend. This may not sound like you now, but it is something that most people do feel like at some stage as they get older, for example as a teenager or an adult. Some people have their first close relationship as a teenager, and some people don't have their first relationship or go out with someone until they're in their twenties. There's no rush, and you shouldn't feel pressure to start having crushes on people or getting into a relationship until you feel ready.

BODY IMAGE

In the **'GET GROWING'** section, we also talked about how boys' bodies change to be different shapes during puberty. All bodies are brilliant, whatever shape or size they are, but for some people, worrying about how their body compares to other people's can be something they think about a lot. They might think a lot about a part of their body they wish they could change, or even look in the mirror and not see themselves for what they truly look like.

Having a healthy body image means accepting your body and the way you look. If you feel good about yourself, then you'll feel happier overall and get more out of life. This will also mean you have good self-esteem, which means you see yourself in a positive light, and as someone worthy of respect from others, which you are! On the flip side, having a negative body image can make you feel low or anxious.

We are all different, and people of all shapes and sizes go on to do amazing things! Try to look at yourself as a whole person, and don't focus on the little bits of yourself you might not like. The way you look is only one small part of what makes you, you. Your personality, achievements, passions and skills are all much more important.

MARCUS RASHFORD
FOOTBALLER
180 centimetres

TOM HOLLAND
ACTOR
173 centimetres

STORMZY
MUSICIAN & ACTIVIST
196 centimetres

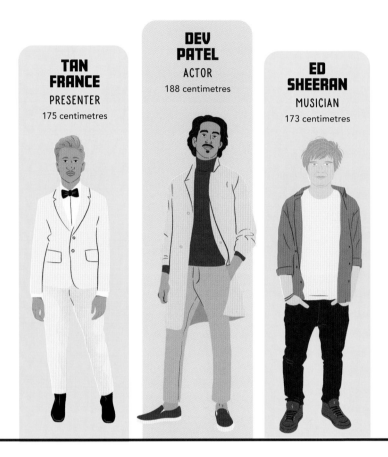

TAN FRANCE
PRESENTER
175 centimetres

DEV PATEL
ACTOR
188 centimetres

ED SHEERAN
MUSICIAN
173 centimetres

SOCIAL MEDIA SAVVY

Social media is brilliant. We can use it to chat to friends, keep up to date with what's going on in the world and be inspired by talented people. However, it does sometimes give us unrealistic expectations for how good a person can look or how amazing their life can be and that can oddly make us feel worse about ourselves, which is never good.

Spending time on social media might make us worry that everyone else has 'better' lives than us – more expensive clothes or bigger houses. We might also compare our bodies. Some boys can worry they are not muscly enough, or too fat or too thin, compared to the people they see online.

ASK DOCTOR EMILY

Q: HOW DOES EVERYONE LOOK SO GOOD ON SOCIAL MEDIA?

A: Social media does not always show reality – often people only share the most flattering pictures, as well as the best and most interesting parts of their lives! Lots of the photos we see online are taken by professional photographers, then edited to change certain things. Spots may have been removed, and body parts might be made to look bigger or smaller.

Social media often focuses too much on appearance, instead of showing all the other things that make someone an amazing human, such as their sense of fun, their kindness, or their funniness. On social media, we can only view photos and videos, which don't often show these more important parts of a person. Instead of worrying about looking a certain way or having a certain lifestyle that might be unachievable, focus on keeping your body and mind healthy and happy and doing things you enjoy with your real-life friends!

STAY SAFE ONLINE

Please remember the golden rules of online life:

Think about waiting until you're 13 to use social media.

Keep your location and personal information private.

Be smart – don't agree to meet face-to-face with an online friend, or send them photos of yourself.

Report anything abusive or that makes you feel uncomfortable to a trusted adult.

Remember your digital footprint – everything you post online is permanent.

My golden rule was to never post something online or send anyone anything I didn't want my mum or dad to see – it seems to have worked well for me! If you are under eighteen, sending photos of private parts of your body is against the law and no one should **EVER** ask you to do that. If they do, report it to your parents or a teacher.

HEALTHY, HAPPY AND ACTIVE

For our brilliant bodies to work as they should, we all
need to do regular exercise and eat well. Eating healthy foods
and keeping active means we have enough energy for our
busy lives. It's all about balance – some foods are useful to our
bodies, helping it get the nutrition it needs for all its different
functions, whereas some are less useful and better to have
as an occasional treat.

HERE ARE SOME TIPS FOR EATING HEALTHILY:

- Eat lots of fruits and vegetables. They're packed with vitamins and minerals that keep your body healthy. You should aim for around five portions a day – a portion is about a handful.

- Be aware of how much sugar you eat. Sugar isn't only in sweets and chocolate, but often hidden in food and drink that looks healthy, like fruit juices and breakfast cereals! Having too much sugar can cause problems like tooth decay, so it's best to save foods high in sugar for an occasional treat, rather than having them every day.

- Drink lots of **WATER**. You need about six to eight cups of water a day to feel at your best, and even more if it's hot or you are exercising. Your body is made of about **60% WATER**, so it needs regular top-ups to replace what you wee or sweat out!

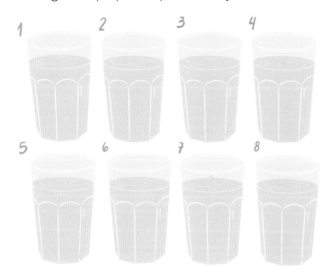

- Eat foods high in **PROTEIN** and **OMEGA-3**. Omega-3 are special types of fat which play an important role in keeping your body healthy. If you eat fish, salmon, tuna and cod are bursting with beneficial Omega-3. If you're vegetarian, eggs, nuts and seeds are an excellent source of protein and also contain Omega-3.

- Watch out for **SATURATED FATS**. We all need some fat in our diet to keep us healthy, but saturated fats aren't good for our bodies. They're in foods like cakes, biscuits and fatty meat, and you should try not to eat too much of them in your day-to-day life.

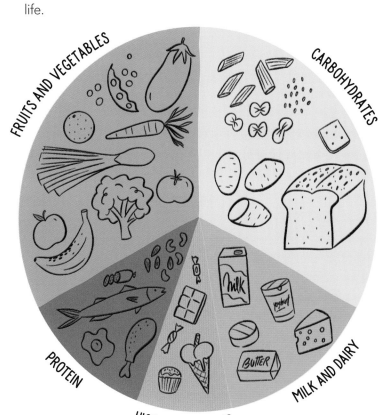

WEIGHT WORRIES?

Food gives us **ENERGY**, which is measured in **CALORIES**. All food has calories in, and how many calories you eat affects how much you weigh. As you go about your day, you use up calories, so it's all about finding a balance between what you put in your body and what your body uses up. If you don't eat enough calories, your body uses up the fat it has stored and you can become **UNDERWEIGHT**. If you take in more calories than your body needs to use, then your body stores these calories as fat and you can become **OVERWEIGHT**. Being very underweight or very overweight as an adult isn't good for you, and can even shorten your life, so it's a great idea to try and get the balance right.

As well as what you eat, how much you weigh will depend on other things, including your height and build. It's not a good idea to compare your weight to your friends', as they are likely to have different body shapes to you! If you do feel worried about your weight, the first thing to do is chat to your parents about it. They might suggest visiting your doctor, who can reassure you that you're healthy, or talk to you about things that could help you lose weight, or put it on, depending on what would be best for your body.

SLEEP SORTED

Just as important as eating right, is **SLEEPING RIGHT!** Getting lots of sleep means you'll have enough energy for your body to grow and develop during puberty. Sleep is vital for your brain, too. It helps you to stay calm in stressful situations, keep focused during lessons and even boosts your mood. You should aim to get about **EIGHT TO TEN HOURS** of sleep a night, although some people need more than this, and some a bit less. If you have the right amount of sleep at night, it should be easy to get out of bed in the morning, and you shouldn't need a nap after school.

GET MOVING

We all know that one of the best things we can do for our bodies is to **EXERCISE**. There are loads of reasons why:

PHYSICAL: exercise builds muscle, strengthens our hearts, improves our blood circulation and builds strong bones.

MENTAL: exercise helps us feel less stressed and anxious. It not only boosts our self-esteem, but it also produces hormones called endorphins, which make us feel happy.

ASK DOCTOR EMILY

Q: HOW CAN I KEEP FIT?

A: Exercise doesn't have to be a chore! Feel free to do fifty push ups if that floats your boat, but you could also try **FOOTBALL, RUGBY, SWIMMING, DANCING, DOG WALKS, SKATEBOARDING, ICE SKATING, TENNIS,** or anything else that regularly gets your body moving and heart pumping!

Playing team sports can help you keep fit and gain some social skills, too. You'll learn how to handle yourself in a group, navigate the highs and lows of tough games and build a super power called 'resilience'. Resilience is the ability to face problems and hard times head on, learn to work your way around them and then bounce back!.

DRUGS, DRINKING AND SMOKING

Becoming more independent is exciting, but with that independence comes **RESPONSIBILITY**. Over the next few years, you'll be faced with lots of difficult choices. It will be up to you to work out which decisions are best for you and your body. Choices you make now might end up having an impact for years to come. For example, you might have friends that start drinking **ALCOHOL, SMOKING CIGARETTES** or **TAKING DRUGS**. You may feel pressure to try them too, even if it's not really what you want to do.

In the UK, if you are under eighteen years old, it is illegal for you to buy alcohol or have alcohol bought for you. It is illegal to take drugs at any age. This means that if you get caught doing these things, you could be **ARRESTED, GET FINED** or **GET A CRIMINAL RECORD**, which might make it harder for you to get a job or travel abroad when you are older. In addition to being illegal, drugs and alcohol are harmful to your body. Drugs can be very dangerous. They can make you ill if you take too much of them, and even put you at risk of dying. There is some evidence that drugs which might be safer for older people can increase the risk of serious mental health problems if you take them when you are younger and your brain is still developing. Many are also addictive, meaning that if you try them a few times, you may find you want to take them again and again, making it difficult to stop taking them. Alcohol can also make you very unwell if you have too much of it, and can change your behaviour so you're more likely to take dangerous risks. It's best to wait until you are legally old enough to try alcohol, then have a small amount at a time to avoid feeling out of control, or being ill the next day.

These days, there's a much better understanding of the dangers of smoking than there was fifty years ago, when lots of people used to do it. Like drugs and alcohol, smoking cigarettes damages your body, filling your lungs with harmful substances and putting pressure on your heart, too. You might have heard that e-cigarettes or vaping aren't as bad for you as smoking, and while that is true, inhaling any chemicals **(IN THIS CASE, NICOTINE, ALONG WITH SOME OTHER CHEMICALS IN VAPE LIQUID)** is not likely to be good for you! Vaping can also be addictive, and sometimes leads people on to smoking cigarettes. It's also such a new thing that more studies need to be done to make sure the chemicals aren't doing damage that we're not aware of yet. **WITH THAT IN MIND, IT'S BEST TO JUST STEER CLEAR!**

YOU DO YOU

The world is made up of all kinds of people. As you go through life, you'll meet friends from different cultures, backgrounds and religions, of all different physical abilities and ages. Another word for the differences between people is **DIVERSITY**. And diversity is something to be celebrated! It would be a very boring world if everyone looked and acted exactly the same! It's important to respect someone wherever they come from, whatever they look like and whatever they believe in.

BE TRUE TO YOURSELF

This book has focused on the **PHYSICAL** and **MENTAL** changes in male bodies and minds. But what does it mean to be male? Male and female are words used to describe somebody's **SEX** – basically which body parts you are born with. If you are born with male body parts, doctors put 'MALE' on your birth certificate. But there's another word we use to talk about being male or female, and that is 'GENDER'. This is slightly different because, while the term 'sex' refers to our bodies, 'GENDER IDENTITY' can refer to how we feel about ourselves, regardless of what body parts we have.

As we discussed earlier in the book, our identities are made up of so much more than what our bodies looks like, so even if you think you know someone's sex or gender from the way they look, you may not be right. It's really important to respect everyone's feelings about who they are. Some people might be born with male body parts, but feel deeply that inside their heart and mind they are female, or vice versa. It can take many years for someone to be sure that their gender identity isn't the same as the sex they were born with. If you feel confused about your identity, then it's important to chat it through with a parent or doctor. In time, things that are really unclear as you're growing up can fall into place and become just 'PART OF YOU', so never hurry yourself to fit into any particular label or group until you really know what you want that label to be.

SUPER SUPPORT NETWORKS

Everybody needs a helping hand or shoulder to cry on sometimes. When we're going through lots of changes, having people around us we can turn to for support or advice is especially important. Take a moment to think about all the people in your life. Make a note in your mind of the friends and family members you know will be there for you, no matter what. **THAT'S YOUR SUPPORT NETWORK!**

As well as your friends and family, you might want to bring people from the wider community into your support network. Some children have social workers, whose job it is to look out for them and their family. School nurses and family doctors can also offer support, particularly if you're worried about your health. Big or small, there's no right or wrong way for a support network to look!

FAMILY SHAPES AND SIZES

There are all kinds of different family set-ups, and your family may look a bit different from some of your friends' families.

Some people live with both their mum and their dad. They might be the only child in the family, or have lots of brothers or sisters, like I do.

Some people live in a single-parent family, just living with either their mum or their dad. Sometimes, they might split their time between both parents, and live in two different homes. Some people live with step-parents. If one or both of their parents have chosen to be with a new partner, they might call them their stepmum or stepdad. If their step-parents have children from previous relationships, then they are usually called stepsisters or stepbrothers. Some people may live with two mums or two dads, in a same-sex parent family.

Some people live in adopted families. You may have heard the term 'ADOPTION' and wondered what it meant. This means the parents who gave birth to a child **(THE BIRTH FAMILY)** were not able to look after them during their childhood. This can be for lots of complicated reasons. Another set of parents **(CALLED THE ADOPTIVE PARENTS)** welcome the child into their own family, where they love and support them as they grow up.

Some people live with **FOSTER PARENTS**. A foster family provides a safe and caring home for a child when birth parents are not able to look after their children. There can be lots of different reasons why this is. Sometimes children are in foster care for a short period of time while temporary problems are sorted out, sometimes it can be for much longer periods of time. Some people who foster children choose to go on to adopt them, so that the children stay with them until they become adults.

That might all sound quite complicated, but the summary is that lots of families work in different ways, and have different mixes of people in them. It is important to accept and understand the differences between us all. We shouldn't be negative or unkind to people who have different family situations to us – they have often had a complicated time getting to their new home set-ups.

PART THREE:

WHAT ABOUT THE GIRLS?

Before we finish, let's have a quick chat about what girls go through during puberty. Puberty usually starts a year or two earlier for girls than it does for boys. While a lot of the changes in boys' bodies are due to the hormone testosterone, in girls' bodies it's the hormone **OESTROGEN** which is more important.

Girls will start to grow **BREASTS** (boobs or bosoms).

HAIR will grow on their legs and arms, under their armpits and in the pubic area.

Like boys, girls go through **GROWTH SPURTS** and get taller.

Girls' **BODY SHAPE CHANGES**. Their hips get wider and they might put weight on in different areas, such as the upper arms and hips.

Some girls might get **SPOTTY SKIN**.

Like boys, **GIRLS GET SWEATIER** during puberty, so often need to start using an antiperspirant.

They will start having **PERIODS**.

WHAT ARE PERIODS?

Just like boys' bodies, girls' bodies change during puberty to get ready to have a baby someday. One way this happens is that hormones trigger the lining of the uterus to get thicker. If a girl doesn't become pregnant, then the lining of the uterus passes out of her body, through the vagina, as a period.

PERIODS happen roughly once a month. Girls' hormones can be up and down at this time, so try to be understanding. If your friend or sister is on their period, be kind and considerate about it, and don't tease them. Periods are a **NATURAL** and **IMPORTANT** part of life and definitely not something to make girls feel embarrassed about!

Each period lasts up to a week, and during this time a small amount of blood will pass out of the vagina. To stop any blood coming through to their clothes, girls wear small pads in their pants called a **'SANITARY TOWEL'**. Sometimes they put a small pad inside the vagina, this is called a **'TAMPON'**.

TAMPON

SANITARY TOWEL

HERE COMES
CONFIDENT YOU!

So, here we are at the end of the book. By now, you should know **EVERYTHING** about growing up. Well, maybe not quite.

Really, to learn everything there is to know about growing up, you have to experience it yourself! You have to go through all those changes – exciting, tricky, confusing or tough – on your own and come out on the other side. I hope you're feeling ready for the adventure.

You've learned about the changes that will happen to your body, from growing facial hair, to your voice deepening and your muscles getting bigger. You've discovered some of the thoughts and feelings you might experience as you go through puberty, and why these might happen. And you've also been given some tips for looking after yourself. **THERE'S A LOT OF INFO CRAMMED IN BETWEEN THE COVERS OF THIS BOOK, SO DO FLICK BACK ANY TIME IF YOU'VE FORGOTTEN SOMETHING.**

If you still have concerns or questions, there are lots of places to go to for advice, and you can find links to some of these at the back of the book. Grown-ups are a good source of knowledge too, as they've already been through all this puberty stuff, so don't feel embarrassed about talking to your parents or a doctor if you're still feeling curious.

Your teenage years can be tricky, but they are also an incredible time where you learn all about the person you will become. When I was starting secondary school, it felt like such a long road ahead – but the time has just flown by! Make the most of your life right now, and try to enjoy the present, even as you get excited about the future.

SO, HERE YOU ARE. CONFIDENT, UNIQUE, AMAZING YOU. THE WORLD IS LUCKY TO HAVE YOU IN IT!

GLOSSARY

Acne A skin condition, also known as 'spots', caused by blocked pores.

Body odour A smell made by bacteria mixing with sweat.

Breasts (boobs) The soft parts on the front of women's and older girls' chests. Women have breasts so they can make milk to feed their babies if they choose to. Boys and men can also have some breast growth, called gynaecomastia.

Emotions Feelings, such as happiness, sadness or anger.

Foreskin The soft skin that covers the sensitive top part of your penis.

Genitals The parts of men and women's bodies which are involved in making babies and going to the toilet. Girls' genitals are mostly on the inside of their bodies and include the uterus (womb), ovaries and vagina. Boys' genitals are mainly on the outside of their bodies and include the testicles and penis.

Glans The top part of the penis that is covered by the foreskin.

Gynaecomastia The enlargement of the breast tissue that some boys can see during their teenage years.

Hormones Chemicals in the body that act like messengers, telling your body what to do and when. Different hormones do different things: some control the way you digest food, some control how and when you grow, and some get your body ready to become an adult.

Ligament A short band of tough tissue that connects bones or supports muscles.

Oestrogen A hormone which plays various roles in the body, including making breast tissue grow in girls.

Ovaries The organs in female bodies which produce egg cells.

Penis The part of male bodies through which sperm and urine are released.

Pituitary gland A little gland in the centre of the brain that organizes the hormones and messages the body needs to go through puberty. It makes everything happen at the right time and in the right order.

Puberty The physical process of your body and mind growing into an adult's.

Pubic hair Hair that grows near your genital area.

Semen Fluid containing sperm.

Sperm Special cells made inside male bodies which, if they meet with an egg in a female body, can grow into a baby.

Testicles (balls) The organs in which sperm cells are made in male bodies.

Testosterone A hormone needed to develop and maintain male sex characteristics, such as facial hair, deep voice and muscle growth.

Uterus (womb) The organ in female bodies where babies grow during pregnancy. It grows as a baby inside it gets bigger.

Vagina A tube inside female bodies that connects the uterus (womb) to the outside of the body.

Wet dream When you accidentally release a bit of semen during your sleep.

USEFUL LINKS

You can find out more about puberty and growing up through the following links. There are also some websites you can visit, or numbers you can call, if you are going through a difficult time and need someone to talk to.

SPOTS AND ACNE

KidsHealth www.kidshealth.org/en/teens/prevent-acne.html

NHS www.nhs.uk/conditions/acne/

PERSONAL HYGIENE AND KEEPING CLEAN

KidsHealth www.kidshealth.org/en/teens/hygiene-basics.html.

BODY IMAGE

CBBC www.bbc.co.uk/cbbc/findoutmore/help-me-out-body-image

HEALTHY LIVING

British Heart Foundation www.bhf.org.uk/informationsupport/support/healthy-living

NHS www.nhs.uk/change4life

MENTAL HEALTH AND EMOTIONAL SUPPORT

Young Minds (Support for children and young people struggling with their mental health) www.youngminds.org.uk
Beat (Support for children and young people suffering with eating disorders) www.beateatingdisorders.co.uk

CALM (Listening services and support for anyone who needs to talk) Helpline: 0800 58 58 58
www.thecalmzone.net

Childline (Support for children and young people in the UK)
Helpline: 0800 1111
www.childline.org.uk

FRANK (Confidential advice and information about drugs, their effects and the law) Helpline: 0300 123 6600
www.talktofrank.com

Happy Maps (A great resource for each age group discussing mental health issues)
www.happymaps.co.uk

INDEX